A large ship has reached its destination far out to sea.

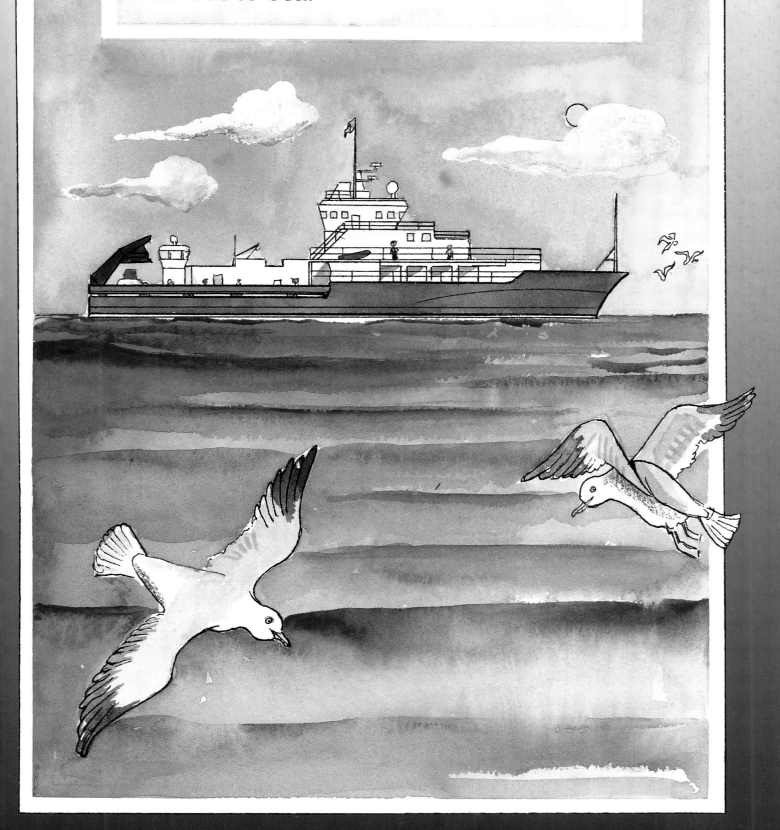

The scientists, oceanographers, and other experts aboard are . . .

Exploring the Deep, Dark Sea

by Gail Gibbons

Little, Brown and Company
Boston   New York   London

TO RANDY MILLER, EXPERT DIVER

*Special thanks to Justine Gardner-Smith, news officer;
Dudley Foster, expedition leader of the* Alvin *group;
and Dr. Judith E. McDowell, scientist at the
Woods Hole Oceanographic Institution,
Woods Hole, Massachusetts*

First Paperback Edition

Library of Congress Cataloging-in-Publication Data

Gibbons, Gail.
  Exploring the deep, dark sea / by Gail Gibbons. — 1st ed.
    p.   cm.
  Summary: Explores the vastly unexplored world beneath the ocean's surface.
  ISBN 0-316-30945-1 (hc) / ISBN 0-316-75549-4 (pb)
  1. Underwater exploration — Juvenile literature. [1. Underwater exploration.
2. Ocean bottom. 3. Marine biology.] I. Title.
GC65.G53 1999
551.46 — dc21   98-14443

HC: 10 9 8 7 6 5 4 3
PB: 10 9 8 7 6 5 4 3 2 1

SC

Printed in Hong Kong

These explorers know that nearly three-fourths of the earth's surface is covered by oceans. And they know that those vast seas can be shallow or as much as 36,000 feet (10,800 meters) deep. The floor of the ocean can be flat for miles, or it can be mountainous. According to this ship's depth finder, the seafloor lies 7,500 feet (2,250 meters) directly below the ship.

pressure-proof hull

ballast

propulsion system

SUBMERSIBLE

manipulator arm

storage

view ports

The weather is clear and calm, perfect conditions for today's mission. Two oceanographers and a pilot climb into a submersible. This small craft is a diving vessel that can measure, videotape, and collect samples of water, plants, and animals found in the ocean. The pilot skillfully maneuvers the submersible wherever the researchers want to go beneath the surface of the ocean.

An **OCEANOGRAPHER** studies the oceans.

Inside, the pilot tests the video cameras, life-support systems, underwater lights, mechanical arms, and all other systems. The hatch closes with a gentle thud. It is fastened and secured. "All systems go!" the pilot announces.

"Prepare to dive!"

The submersible is lifted and moved out over the water, where it is lowered and released. At first it bobs on the sea's surface. Then, as water flows into the ballast tanks, the submersible slowly sinks away from its mother ship in a mass of bubbles.

What an amazing view! Rays of sunlight flash through the warm, blue water. The submersible drops about 100 feet (30.5 meters) per minute. "Two hundred feet...," the pilot says into a microphone, transmitting their depth to the mother ship.

JELLYFISH

HERRING

MACKEREL

THE SUNLIGHT ZONE

The submersible is in the sunlight zone, the area from the water's surface to about 450 feet (150 meters) below. In this shallow part of the ocean, sunlight supports many forms of plant life, both big and small. This is where most marine plants, fish, and other sea creatures live.

PORPOISE

TIGER SHARK

TUNA

A **HUMPBACK WHALE** is a mammal.

COD

A **MAMMAL** gives birth to its young. Other creatures lay eggs.

All living things are part of the world's food chain. The oceanic part of the food chain includes the tiniest plants and fish up to the largest marine mammals. Their survival depends on one another. As the submersible continues to sink, with sea creatures darting about, the sea begins to grow darker and colder.

"Four hundred fifty feet..."

DOLPHIN

SKATE

THE TWILIGHT ZONE

The small craft now passes into the twilight zone, from 450 feet (150 meters) to 3,300 feet (1,000 meters) down. At first, the water here is a very dark blue. Sunlight fades. It is too dark and too cold here for plants to grow. "Look! A squid!" calls out one of the researchers.

JELLYFISH

SQUID

BLACK STAR-EATER

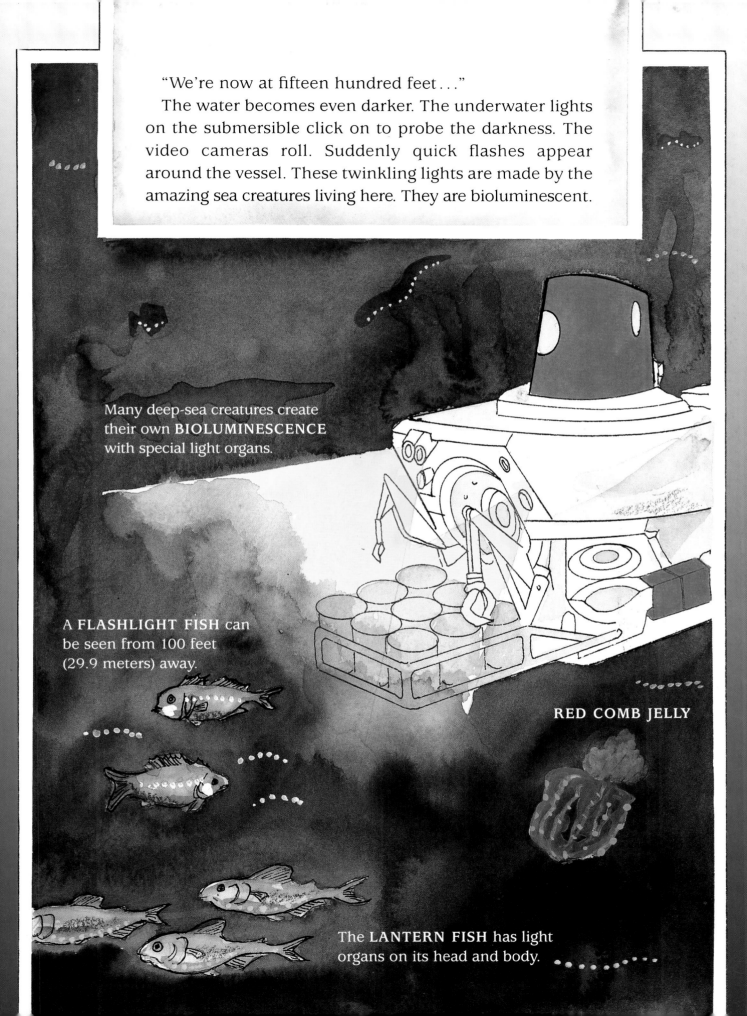

"We're now at fifteen hundred feet..."

The water becomes even darker. The underwater lights on the submersible click on to probe the darkness. The video cameras roll. Suddenly quick flashes appear around the vessel. These twinkling lights are made by the amazing sea creatures living here. They are bioluminescent.

Many deep-sea creatures create their own **BIOLUMINESCENCE** with special light organs.

A **FLASHLIGHT FISH** can be seen from 100 feet (29.9 meters) away.

RED COMB JELLY

The **LANTERN FISH** has light organs on its head and body.

These creatures of the twilight zone use their bioluminescence to survive. Some send out light patterns to
attract mates. Others blind their predators with quick
flashes of light. Some camouflage themselves by using
light organs on their undersides to blend in with any light
flickering from above. As many as four-fifths of all
creatures in the oceans are bioluminescent.

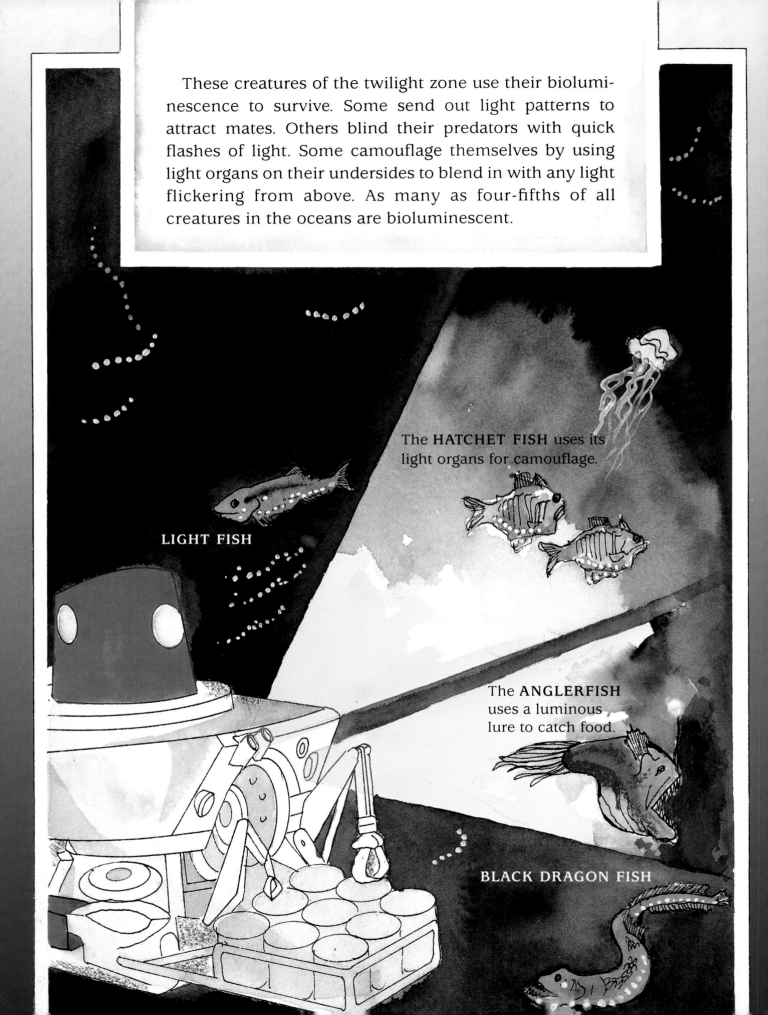

The **HATCHET FISH** uses its
light organs for camouflage.

LIGHT FISH

The **ANGLERFISH**
uses a luminous
lure to catch food.

BLACK DRAGON FISH

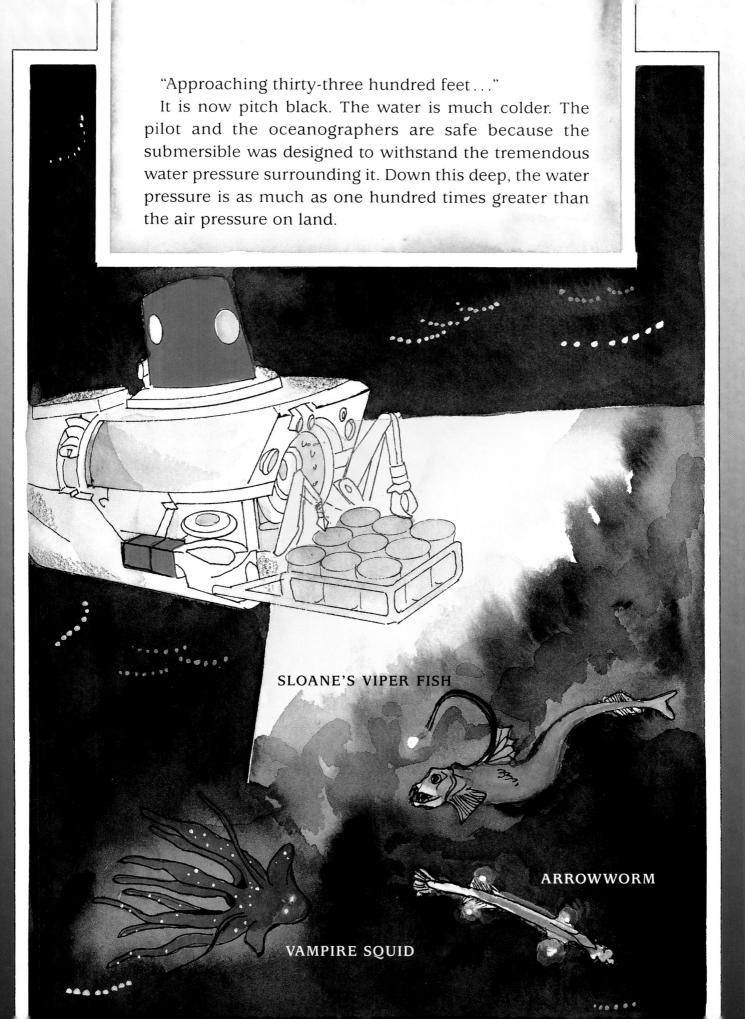

"Approaching thirty-three hundred feet..."

It is now pitch black. The water is much colder. The pilot and the oceanographers are safe because the submersible was designed to withstand the tremendous water pressure surrounding it. Down this deep, the water pressure is as much as one hundred times greater than the air pressure on land.

SLOANE'S VIPER FISH

ARROWWORM

VAMPIRE SQUID

THE DARK ZONE

"It's amazing down here!" the pilot reports. "We're at forty-five hundred feet, and we're gathering samples." The dark zone lies between 3,300 feet (1,000 meters) and 13,000 feet (3,900 meters) below the water's surface. Some of the creatures moving about look weird and scary. Some are hunters. Others are scavengers, eating what floats down from above.

DRAGON FISH

VIPER FISH

DEEP-SEA ANGLERFISH

SNIPE EEL

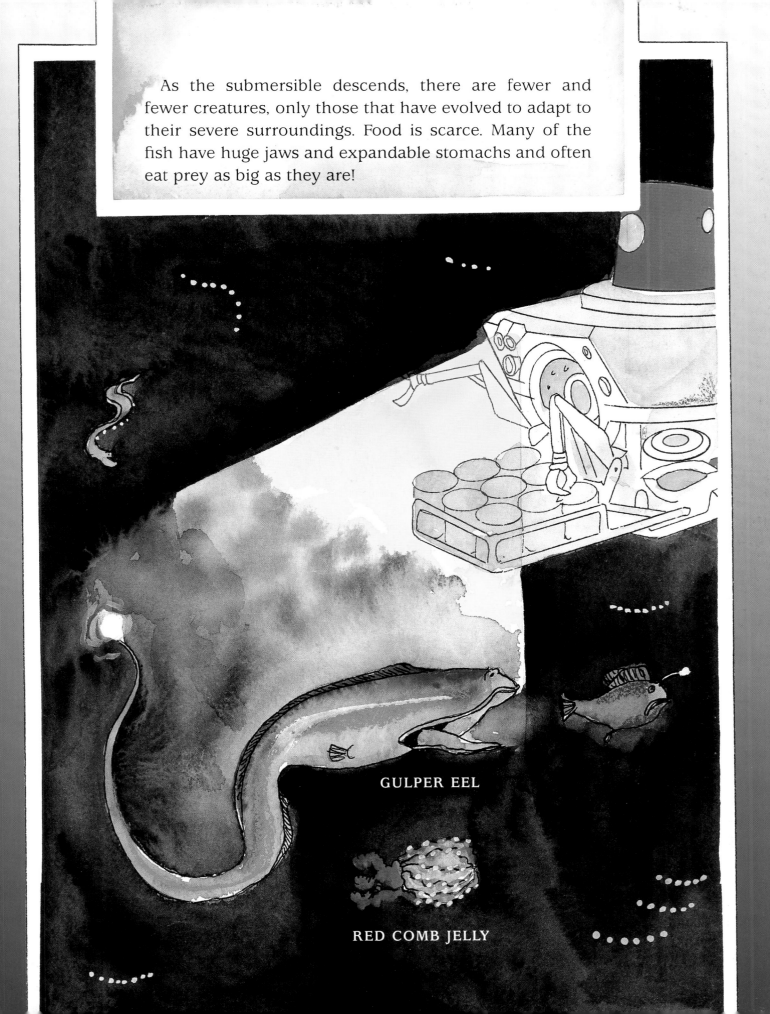

As the submersible descends, there are fewer and fewer creatures, only those that have evolved to adapt to their severe surroundings. Food is scarce. Many of the fish have huge jaws and expandable stomachs and often eat prey as big as they are!

GULPER EEL

RED COMB JELLY

At last the submersible nears the ocean floor.
"Five thousand feet..."

"Six thousand feet..."

"Seven thousand feet..."

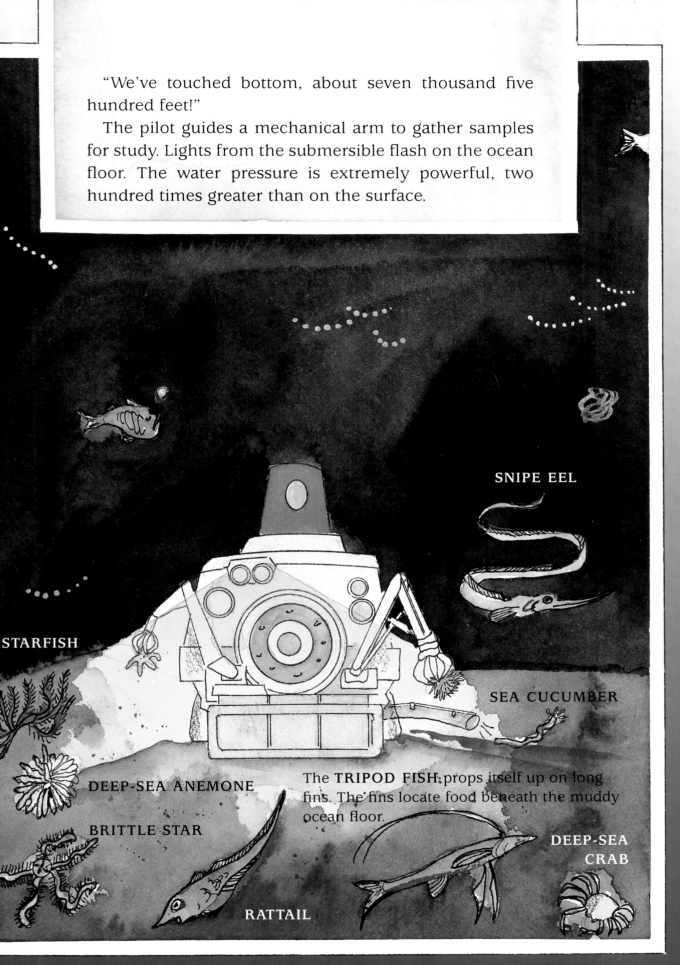

"We've touched bottom, about seven thousand five hundred feet!"

The pilot guides a mechanical arm to gather samples for study. Lights from the submersible flash on the ocean floor. The water pressure is extremely powerful, two hundred times greater than on the surface.

SNIPE EEL

STARFISH

SEA CUCUMBER

DEEP-SEA ANEMONE

The **TRIPOD FISH** props itself up on long fins. The fins locate food beneath the muddy ocean floor.

BRITTLE STAR

DEEP-SEA CRAB

RATTAIL

The researchers collect specimens until all the sample containers are full. They also take numerous still photos. The video cameras continue to run.

BASKET SPONGE

URCHIN

SUN STAR

SEA CUCUMBER

BRITTLE STAR

DEEP-SEA PRAWN

In about four hours the research is complete.

The pilot radios the mother ship that it is time to surface. The submersible steadily makes its ascent. The water changes from black . . . to dark blue . . . to light shades of green and blue until . . .

The submersible breaks through the surface of the smooth ocean waters. A cable is attached to the craft. It is lifted from the sea to the ship's deck. The hatch is opened, and the passengers climb out. Mission accomplished!

Everyone on board the ship gathers around to see what was retrieved from down below. The specimens will be cleaned, identified, and studied in the ship's lab. The photos and videotapes will be viewed. What new discoveries will be made this time?

THE ABYSS

Maybe next time the crew will explore even deeper parts of the ocean. Below the dark zone is the abyss, between 13,000 feet (3,900 meters) and 20,000 feet (6,000 meters). Some submersibles can go as deep as 22,000 feet (6,600 meters). To go deeper, unmanned ROVs, or remotely operated vehicles, are used. Some of them are small enough to slip into tight spaces.

DEEP-SEA SQUID

GLASS SPONGES

SEA SPIDER

BRITTLE STAR

SEA P

ROVs are remotely controlled by cable from a submersible or ship. They are equipped with manipulator arms, powerful lights, and cameras that send images directly to the mother ship. The few creatures living in the abyss have soft, squishy bodies. They don't need the protection of strong skin and bones because the water is so still at this depth.

RATTAIL

The **ABYSSAL PLAINS** cover almost half of the deep sea floor.

SEA CUCUMBER

DEEP-SEA ANEMONE

THE TRENCHES

Below the abyss, beginning at 20,000 feet (6,000 meters), is where deep cracks in the ocean floor, called trenches, are found. The Marianas Trench, in the Pacific Ocean, is the deepest part of all the oceans, 36,200 feet (11,033 meters) deep!

DEEP-SEA ANEMONE

POLYCHAETE WORM

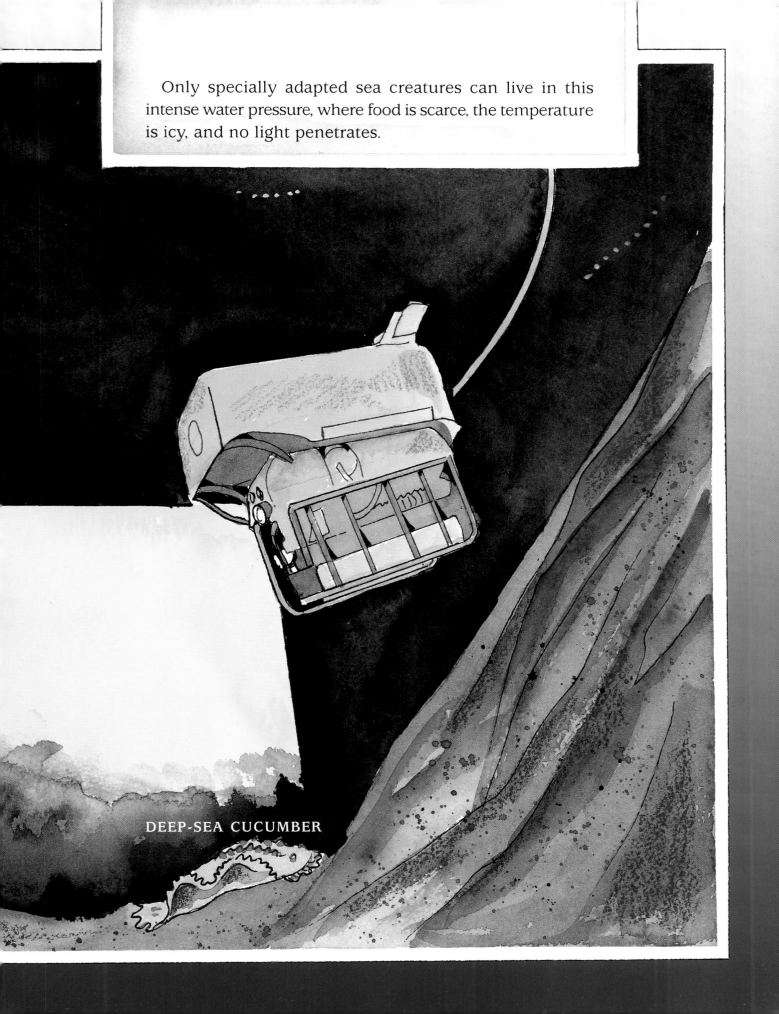

Only specially adapted sea creatures can live in this intense water pressure, where food is scarce, the temperature is icy, and no light penetrates.

DEEP-SEA CUCUMBER

Not long ago, people believed that the deep oceans and the ocean beds were lifeless. How could anything survive in the endless blackness?

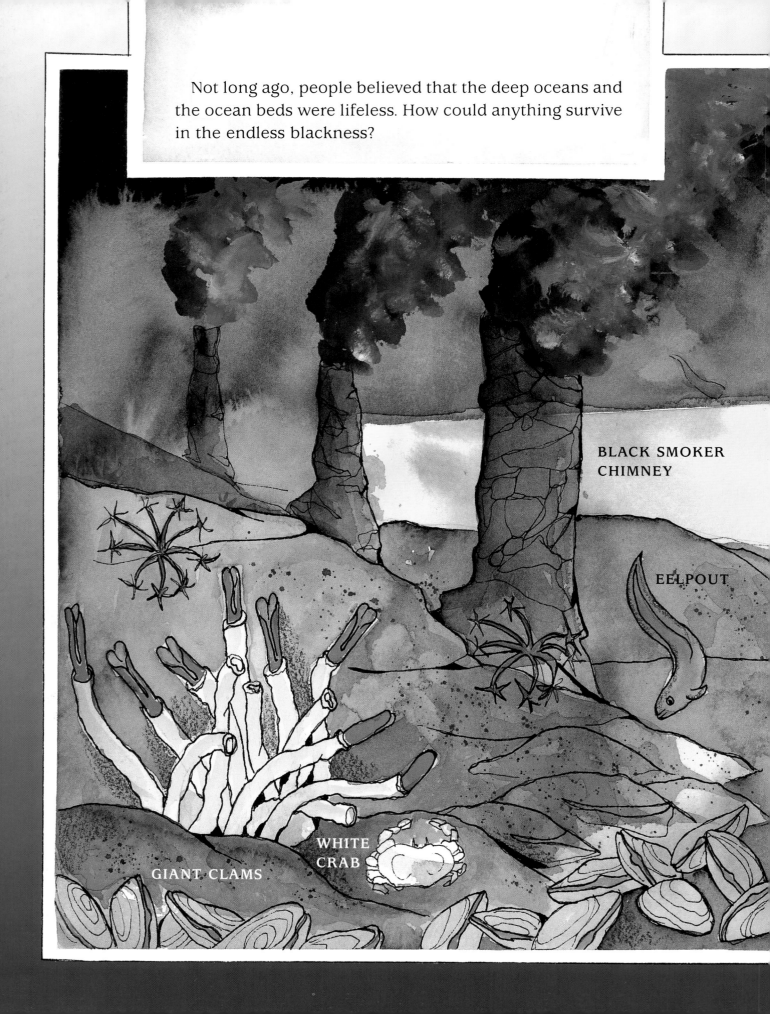

BLACK SMOKER
CHIMNEY

EELPOUT

WHITE
CRAB

GIANT CLAMS

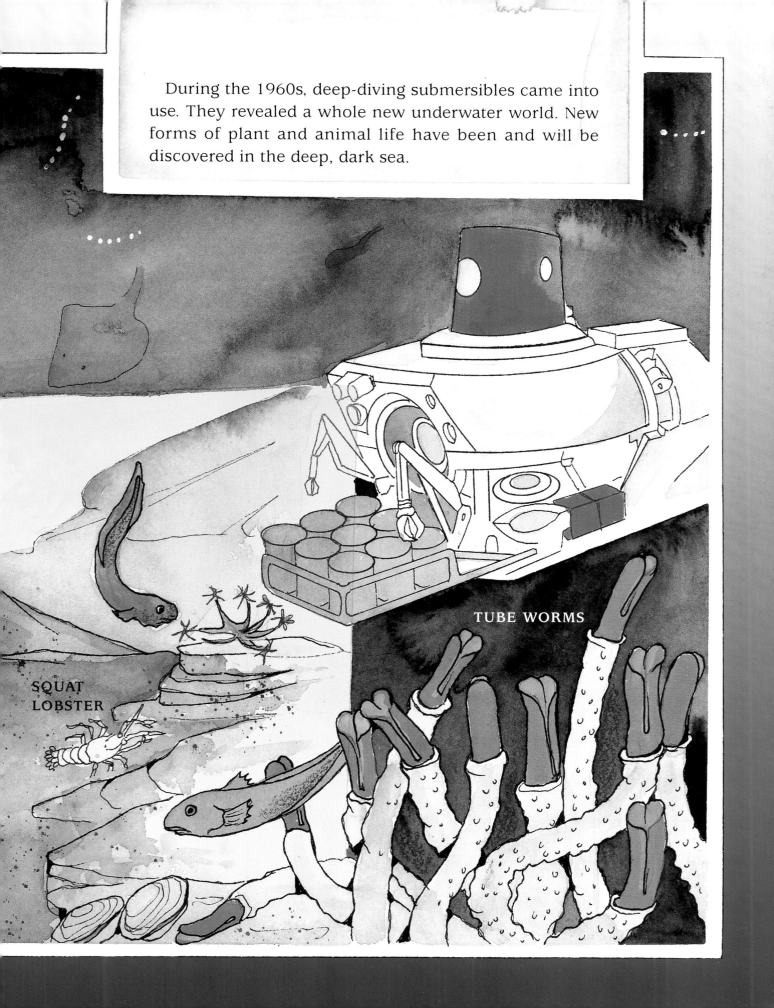

During the 1960s, deep-diving submersibles came into use. They revealed a whole new underwater world. New forms of plant and animal life have been and will be discovered in the deep, dark sea.

SQUAT
LOBSTER

TUBE WORMS

DIVING . . . PAST AND PRESENT

At first

Divers dove without any equipment. They held their breath while gathering sponges, oysters, and other creatures from shallow areas.

1250

The diving bell was invented. Air was trapped in the top of the bell. The diver could breathe until the air supply ran out.

1715

An Englishman, John Lethbridge, used one of the first diving units, a wooden cylinder with a glass view port. He went about 60 feet (18.3 meters) deep.

1930

Dr. William Beebe and Otis Barton dove to 1,428 feet (435.3 meters) in a bathysphere, a diving sphere for deep-sea observation, off the coast of Bermuda.

1942

The Aqua-Lung was invented by Jacques-Yves Cousteau and Emile Gagnan. Divers could now stay underwater longer and move freely, because they carried their air supply in a tank on their backs.

1830

The first diving suit was used. A flexible tube connected the helmet to an air pump on deck.

1892

Louis Boutan took the first underwater photographs off the coast of France. He lowered his camera 165 feet (50.3 meters) deep.

1960

Trieste, a bathyscaphe, or deep-diving vessel attached beneath a large cylindrical hull, went to the deepest part of the ocean, the Marianas Trench. It descended 35,800 feet (10,900 meters).

1989

The ROV *Jason Jr.* was launched from *Alvin* to make the historic exploration of the ship-wrecked *Titanic.*

The Japanese submersible *Shinkai-6500* went to the depth of 21,325 feet (6,397 meters). It is the world's deepest diving submersible.

The Future

A new submersible, called *Deep Flight,* is being developed. It is lowered by thrusters and will be able to "fly" to the deepest part of the oceans.

THE DEEP, DARK SEA

Until two hundred years ago, people thought many parts of the ocean were bottomless.

At one time, sailors believed that sea monsters lurked in the ocean, waiting to attack.

About five hundred years ago, the Italian artist Leonardo da Vinci designed a device for breathing underwater, although he never tried it.

A giant squid can be up to sixty-six feet (twenty meters) long.

About twenty years ago, hydrothermal vents were discovered. Tube worms and giant clams live around these vents, where hot lava, or melted rock, seeps up through cracks in the ocean floor. They are very hot —662°F (350°C).

Sometimes minerals in the hot water around thermal vents form large chimneys, sometimes as tall as a two-story building. The water rushing out of the chimneys is as black as smoke.

Creatures that live in the deep sea are rarely more than one foot (30 centimeters) long.

We know less about many parts of the oceans today than we know about the surface of the moon.

Ninety-eight percent of the ocean floor is still unexplored.